SUPER SIMPLE BODY

INSIDE YOUR GERMS

KARIN HALVORSON, M.D.
Consulting Editor, Diane Craig, M.A./Reading Specialist

Super Sandcastle

An Imprint of Abdo Publishing
abdopublishing.com

VISIT US AT ABDOPUBLISHING.COM

Published by Abdo Publishing, a division of ABDO, PO Box 398166, Minneapolis, Minnesota 55439. Copyright © 2016 by Abdo Consulting Group, Inc. International copyrights reserved in all countries. No part of this book may be reproduced in any form without written permission from the publisher. Super SandCastle™ is a trademark and logo of Abdo Publishing.

Printed in the United States of America,
North Mankato, Minnesota
102015
012016

**THIS BOOK CONTAINS
RECYCLED MATERIALS**

Editor: Liz Salzmann
Content Developer: Nancy Tuminelly
Cover and Interior Design: Mighty Media, Inc.
Photo Credits: Shutterstock

Library of Congress Cataloging-in-Publication Data
Halvorson, Karin, 1979- author.
  Inside your germs / Karin Halvorson, M.D. ; consulting editor, Diane Craig, M.A./reading specialist.
    pages cm. -- (Super simple body)
  ISBN 978-1-62403-944-7
1. Human physiology--Juvenile literature. 2. Human biology--Juvenile literature. 3. Host-bacteria relationships--Juvenile literature. 4. Bacteria--Juvenile literature. 5. Viruses--Juvenile literature. I. Title. II. Series: Halvorson, Karin, 1979- Super simple body.
  QP37.H325 2016
  612--dc23
                        2015020590

Super SandCastle™ books are created by a team of professional educators, reading specialists, and content developers around five essential components—phonemic awareness, phonics, vocabulary, text comprehension, and fluency—to assist young readers as they develop reading skills and strategies and increase their general knowledge. All books are written, reviewed, and leveled for guided reading and early reading intervention programs for use in shared, guided, and independent reading and writing activities to support a balanced approach to literacy instruction.

NOTE TO ADULTS

THIS BOOK is all about encouraging children to learn the science of how their bodies work! Be there to help make science fun and interesting for young readers. Many activities are included in this book to help children further explore what they've learned. Some require adult assistance and/or permission. Make sure children have appropriate places where they can do the activities safely.

Children may also have questions about what they've learned. Offer help and guidance when they have questions. Most of all, encourage them to keep exploring and learning new things!

CONTENTS

YOUR BODY

You're amazing! So is your body!
Your body has a lot of different parts. Your
kidneys, skin, blood, muscles, and bones
all work together every day. They keep you
moving. Even when you don't realize it.

Your body protects itself from the outside world. It even protects you from things you cannot see, such as germs. Some germs can grow in your body. They make you sick. Your body works to keep you safe.

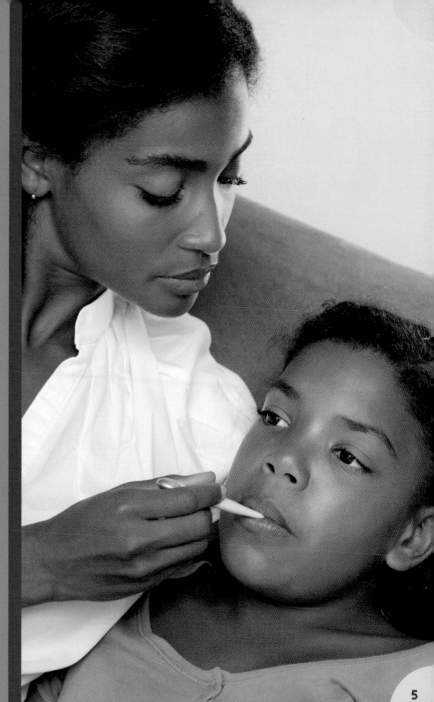

ALL ABOUT GERMS

Germs are tiny living organisms. They are everywhere. They live in you and on you. They are even in the air you breathe.

Most germs are so small you need a microscope to see them.

BACTERIA

VIRUSES

Four Types of Germs

BACTERIA (*BAK-teer-ee-uh*) each have only one cell. Bacteria get food from their surroundings.

VIRUSES (*VYE-ruhs-ez*) grow inside other living things. They take over cells.

FUNGI (*FUHN-gye*) are like plants. They are made of many cells.

PROTOZOA (*proh-tuh-ZOH-uh*) are also one-cell organisms. They live in liquid.

FUNGI

PROTOZOA

ARE THERE GOOD GERMS?

Some bacteria keep you healthy. Your gut is full of helpful bacteria. They break down food and keep out bad bacteria. Some bacteria make **vitamins**.

FAST FACT

The biggest type of bacteria is about the size of a period.

Spreading Germs

Germs need a body to survive. They move from body to body.
They have a few tricks to move quickly. They can spread in several ways.

How Germs Spread

BY TOUCH

THROUGH THE AIR

IN DIRTY WATER

IN SPOILED FOOD

IN BODY LIQUIDS

GLITTER GERMS

WATCH HOW GERMS SPREAD!

WHAT YOU NEED: SMALL BOTTLE OF HAND SANITIZER, FUNNEL, MEASURING SPOONS, 1 TEASPOON GLITTER, STOPWATCH

HOW TO DO IT

1. Use the funnel to put the glitter in the sanitizer bottle.

2. Put the cap back on tightly. Shake the bottle to mix in the glitter.

3. Rub a small amount of hand sanitizer on your hands.

4. Watch the glitter come off on things you touch throughout the day. Make a note of where the glitter turns up!

5. Wash your hands with soap and water. Time how long it takes to get the glitter off.

WHAT'S HAPPENING?

The glitter spreads like germs spread. It can be hard to get off even when you wash your hands well. The glitter is easy to spread around if it isn't washed off. Just like germs!

INCREDIBLE
CELLS

Every plant, animal, and bacteria is made of cells. They are the building blocks of every living thing. Most germs are one cell.

A cell has an outer wall. Inside the wall is cytoplasm (*SYE-tuh-plaz-uhm*). This is a special liquid.

ANIMAL CELL

CYTOPLASM

NUCLEUS

ORGANELLES

The working parts of the cell float in the liquid. They are called organelles (*OR-guh-nelz*). The organelles make energy and store **proteins**.

Animal and plant cells have a brain. It's called the nucleus (*NOO-klee-uhs*).

PLANT CELL

NUCLEUS

CYTOPLASM

ORGANELLES

BACTERIA CELL

Germs can get into a cell. They sneak through the cell wall. Then they use the cell to make more germs.

ORGANELLES

JUST EAT IT!

MAKE AN EDIBLE CELL!

WHAT YOU NEED: PARCHMENT PAPER, BAKING SHEET, CUTTING BOARD, KNIFE, PRE-MADE COOKIE DOUGH, OVEN MITT, FROSTING, SPRINKLES, SMALL AND ROUND CANDIES

HOW TO DO IT

1. Cover the baking sheet with parchment paper. Unwrap the cookie dough. Put it on a cutting board. Cut the dough into ½-inch (1.25 cm) slices. Place them on the baking sheet. Bake according to the directions on the package. Let the cookies cool.

2. Put frosting in the center of a cookie. Leave the edge plain.

3. Put sprinkles on the frosting.

4. Put a candy on the frosting.

5. Repeat steps 2 through 4 with the rest of the cookies.

WHAT'S HAPPENING?

The edge of the cookie is the cell wall. The frosting is the cytoplasm. The sprinkles are the organelles. The candy is the nucleus.

BACTERIA

Bacteria live everywhere. They are in the soil. They are on your teeth. You can find them in the kitchen and the bathroom.

Bacteria are some of the oldest living things on the planet. Many are good for you. But some make you sick.

Divide and Conquer

Bacteria spread by dividing. Some split in half. **Billions** of bacteria are made every day.

Fire and Ice

Bacteria are tough. They are found in boiling water and inside ice in the **Antarctic**.

Strep Throat

Strep throat is one **infection** caused by a bacteria. The bacteria is called streptococcus (*STREP-tuh-kahk-uhs*). Antibacterial medicines help your body kill bacteria.

CLOSE-UP OF STREPTOCOCCUS BACTERIA

DO THE SPLITS!

MAKE LIKE BACTERIA AND SPLIT!

WHAT YOU NEED: SHEET OF PAPER, MARKER, SCISSORS

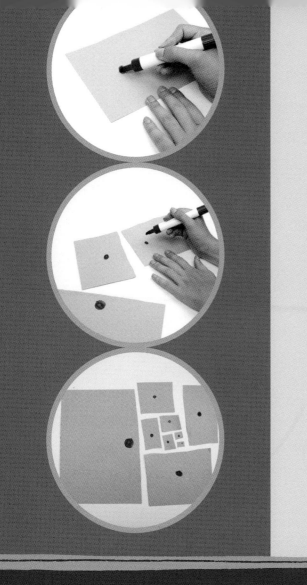

HOW TO DO IT

1. Draw a dot on the paper.

2. Cut the paper in half. Draw a dot on the blank half.

3. Cut both halves in two. Draw a dot on each of the blank pieces.

4. Keep cutting the pieces of paper in half. Draw dots on the blank pieces. How many dots can you make?

WHAT'S HAPPENING?

Each piece of paper is a bacteria cell. The dots are the nuclei. Bacteria cells split in half. They make copies. It is how they spread. Bacteria can make up to 1,024 copies in 5 hours!

VIRUSES

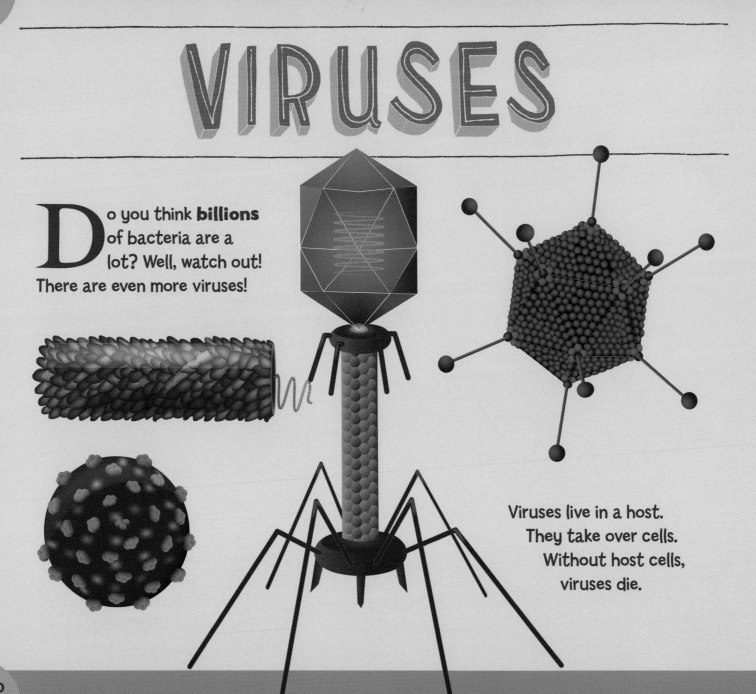

Do you think **billions** of bacteria are a lot? Well, watch out! There are even more viruses!

Viruses live in a host. They take over cells. Without host cells, viruses die.

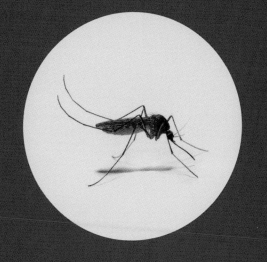

MOSQUITO

Viruses can be found in many creatures, from **mosquitoes** to humans. You have probably caught a human virus before. It is the common cold!

Viruses are always changing. That's how they survive.

FUNGI

Fungi come in many shapes and sizes. They like warm, wet places. Some fungi are too small to see with your eyes. Others are a little bigger.

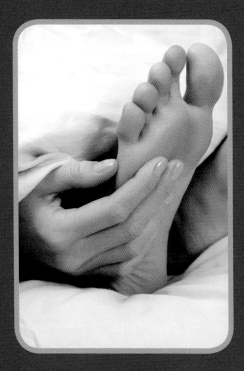

Fungi cause athlete's foot. It's an **itchy rash**.

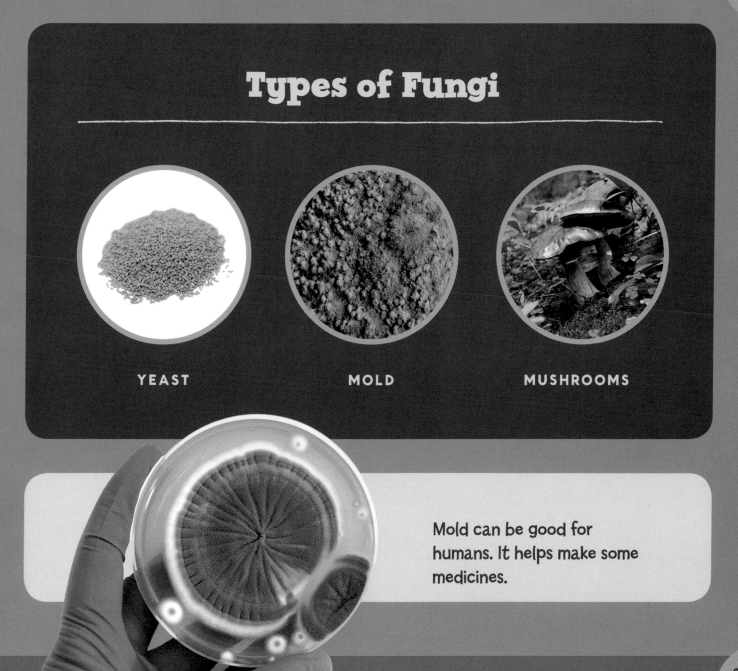

Types of Fungi

YEAST

MOLD

MUSHROOMS

Mold can be good for humans. It helps make some medicines.

GERM DETECTIVE

HUNT GERMS IN YOUR HOUSE!

WHAT YOU NEED: 4 PLASTIC CUPS, MARKER, MIXING BOWL, MEASURING CUPS AND SPOONS, ½ CUP BOILING WATER, 2 TEASPOONS SUGAR, 2 TEASPOONS GELATIN, MIXING SPOON, PLASTIC WRAP, 3 COTTON SWABS

HOW TO DO IT

1 Label the cups 1 through 4. Mix the water, sugar, and gelatin in a bowl. Pour about 1 inch (2.5 cm) of the mixture into each cup. Cover the cups with plastic wrap. Put them in the refrigerator for 1 day.

2 Take the cups out of the refrigerator. Wipe a cotton swab on the table. Rub the swab on the gelatin in cup number 2. Wipe a new cotton swab on the inside of your mouth. Rub it on the gelatin in cup number 3.

3 Wipe a new cotton swab in the kitchen sink. Rub it on the gelatin in cup number 4. Don't rub anything on the gelatin in cup number 1. Cover the cups with plastic wrap again. Set them in a dark corner. After 5 days, look at what has grown on the gelatin.

WHAT'S HAPPENING?

Germs grow when they have food. The gelatin is food for bacteria. The more germs a swab had, the faster the bacteria grew. Which cup had the most stuff growing in it? That swab had the most germs!

PROTOZOA

Protozoa live in liquid. They move with special tails called flagella (*fluh-JEL-uh*). There are many types of protozoa.

FLAGELLA

Some protozoa can make people sick. One of them is malaria (*muh-LAIR-ee-uh*).

Protozoa live in water and blood. **Mosquitoes** can give humans these germs by biting them.

RED BLOOD
CELL INFECTED
WITH MALARIA

GERM
WARRIORS

Your body works to protect you from germs! It has many ways to keep you from getting sick.

• Skin is a wall. It keeps germs from getting inside your body.

• **Mucus** traps germs in a sticky liquid.

• Tears wash away things that get into your eyes.

• The acids in your stomach kill germs you eat or drink.

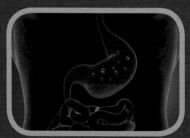

Vaccines

Don't be afraid of needles! Needles give you vaccine (*VAK-seen*) shots. Vaccines protect you from germs. Vaccines teach cells what bad germs look like. If the germs get in your body, the cells kill them before you get sick!

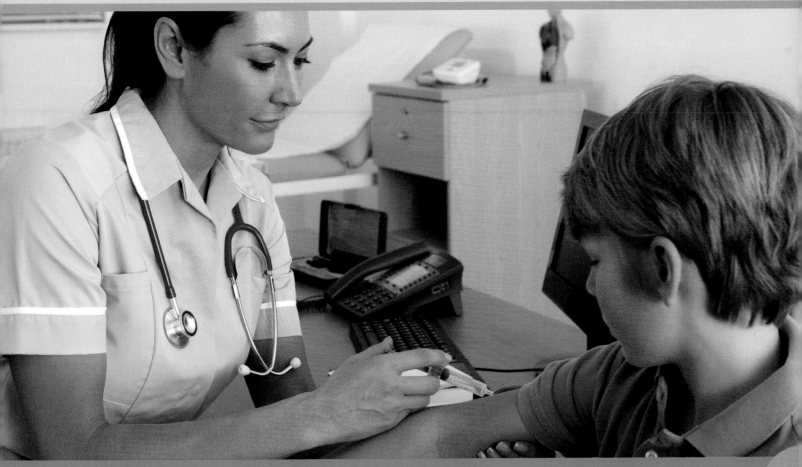

PREVENTION

ou can do a lot to keep
unhealthy germs out of
your body!

WASH YOUR HANDS OFTEN.

**COVER YOUR NOSE AND MOUTH
WHEN YOU COUGH AND SNEEZE.**

EAT A HEALTHY DIET.

PLAY AND BE ACTIVE.

GET A GOOD NIGHT'S REST.

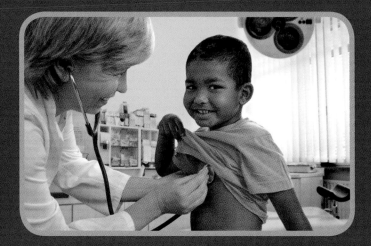

GO TO THE DOCTOR EVERY
YEAR FOR A CHECKUP.

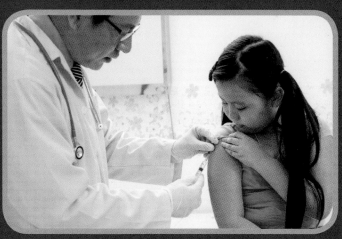

KEEP YOUR VACCINES UP TO DATE.

GLOSSARY

ANTARCTIC – the area around the South Pole.

BILLION – a very large number. One billion is also written 1,000,000,000.

INFECTION – a disease caused by the presence of bacteria or other germs.

ITCH – an uncomfortable feeling on your skin that makes you want to scratch.

KIDNEY – an organ in the body that turns waste from the blood into urine.

MOSQUITO – an insect with two wings that bites people to drink their blood.

MUCUS – a slippery, sticky substance produced by the body.

PROTEIN – a combination of certain kinds of chemical elements. Proteins are found in all plant and animal cells.

RASH – a skin condition with red spots that can be painful or itchy.

VITAMIN – a substance needed for good health, found naturally in plants and meats.